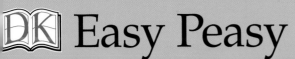

Easy Peasy
CHINESE
Workbook

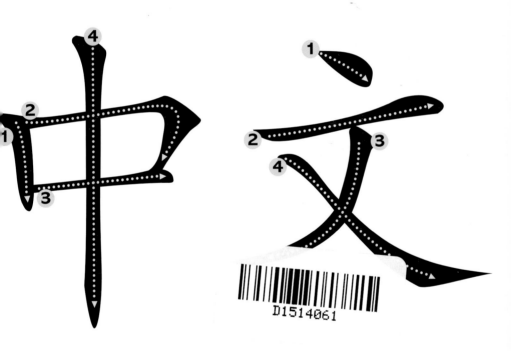

Mandarin Chinese
practice for beginners

Author Elinor Greenwood
Consultant Katharine Carruthers
Art Editors Emma Hobson, Hoa Luc
Editor Cécile Landau
Art Director Martin Wilson
Publishing Manager Bridget Giles
Producer, pre-production Francesca Wardell
Producer Christine Ni

First published in Great Britain in 2015 by
Dorling Kindersley Limited,
80 Strand, London, WC2R 0RL

A CIP catalogue record for this book
is available from the British Library

ISBN 978-0-2411-8495-0

Printed and bound in China

A WORLD OF IDEAS:
SEE ALL THERE IS TO KNOW

www.dk.com

Contents

加油!

Jiā yóu!
Go for it!

Contents **3**

Foreword

This is a workbook, and learning Chinese is the mission. Here are five tips to help.

1 Take the chance to practise when you can.
Nǐ hǎo!

2 Go slow. Half an hour a day is better than two straight hours.

3 Test yourself. Make flashcards and doodle characters in spare moments.

4 Go back on yourself; repeat, repeat and check it's all gone in.

5 Practice makes perfect, so using this workbook is a great start.

太好了!
Fantastic!

Top ten most common Chinese characters

These are all in the book...

1 de   possessive particle   的   **6** rén   person   人

2 yī   one   一   **7** wǒ   I   我

3 shì   to be   是   **8** zài   at   在

4 bù   no/not   不   **9** yǒu   to have   有

5 le   verb particle   了   **10** tā   he   他

A companion book

This workbook is a companion book to *Easy Peasy Chinese* [available at all good booksellers]. All the pronunciations are available on the CD attached to that book.

Using the workbook

Although it is a 'work' book, it's also fun! There is space to doodle and draw, as well as other fun stuff. It features:

- Memory tips and pinyin practice
- How to write all the characters with clear stroke order
- Key characters that you won't forget
- Squared paper to practise what you learn at the end of each section
- Pronunciation tips, too

Keeping it simple

This book includes useful and commonly used Chinese characters. The information is not overwhelming, with a pace of roughly six characters per double-page spread.

Remember, the secret of learning Chinese is:

 Màn màn lái!
Take it easy!

Pinyin and tones

Chinese has no alphabet. The written language is Chinese characters. These give no clue to pronunciation, so a pronunciation guide has developed in Roman letters. This is called pinyin.

For example: 中文 is written **Zhōngwén** in pinyin.

Tones and tone marks

Mandarin Chinese has four tones, and one 'toneless' tone. The tone you use when pronouncing each one-syllable sound determines the meaning. The tone marks ¯ ´ ˇ ` on the vowel show which tone to use.

Here is how to pronounce the different tones:

1ˢᵗ tone high level

Pitch your voice high and hold the sound there slightly longer than seems natural.

mā

mother

As a doctor tells you when looking down your throat
Say:

Aaah!

2ⁿᵈ tone rising

From the middle level of your voice range to the top. Raise your eyebrows as you say it!

má

hemp

Like the tone at the end of a question.

What?

Numbering the tones

The tones are numbered, and when you are learning Chinese, it is good to know which tone is which number.

Practise by writing the tone marks on these pinyin words:

3rd tone:	mi	4th tone:	mi	1st tone:	mi
1st tone:	zhū	2nd tone:	zhú	3rd tone:	zhǔ
4th tone:	bà	1st tone:	bā	2nd tone:	bá

3rd tone falling then rising

From the middle level, down deep, then up a bit.

mǎ

horse

Like when you're surprised.

Really?

4th tone falling

A short, sharp fall from your high voice pitch. Stamp your foot as you say it!

mà

scold

The tone of a statement.

No!

Different strokes

Chinese characters are not random squiggles. They are made up of set strokes.

Copy these strokes in the boxes provided. Follow the direction of the arrows.

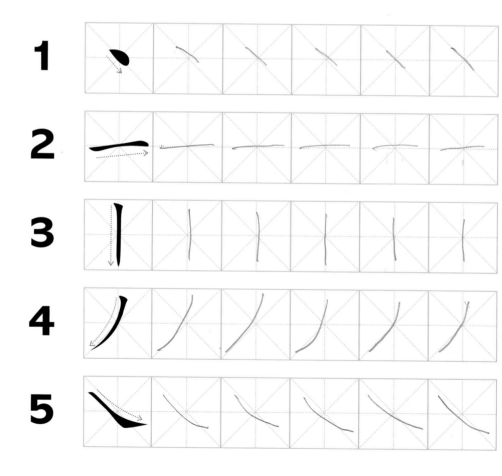

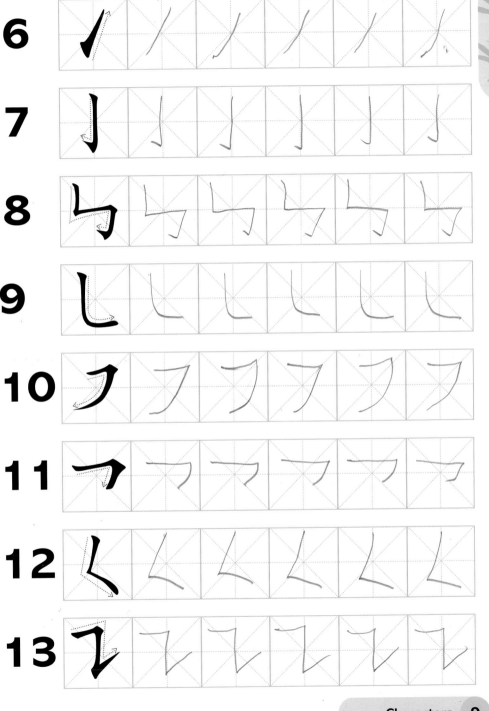

Stroke order

The characters are arranged in a set way, too. Follow the correct stroke order to write beautiful characters.

Follow the numbered strokes to write the characters. The two general rules are:

1 **Write top to bottom**

三
sān
three

Trace Freehand

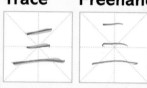

2 **And left to right**

川
chuān
river

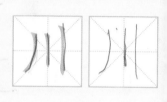

Practise writing these characters using the above two rules:

上
shàng
on/above

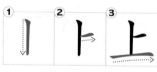
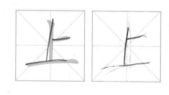

拉
lā
to pull

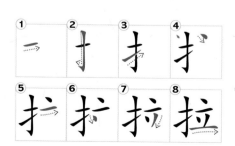

Common variations

There are variations, however. It depended on what made less splodges when scholars first wrote with brushes and ink long ago.

Here are some examples...

Horizontal before vertical

十

shí
ten

Outside then inside

月
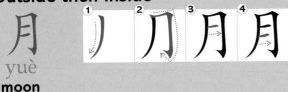

yuè
moon

Centre before outside

小
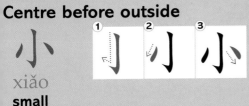

xiǎo
small

Left vertical first

口
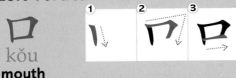
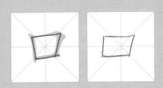

kǒu
mouth

Bottom horizontal last

王
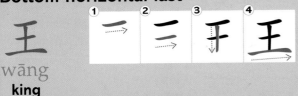

wāng
king

Mixing it up

In any block of Chinese text, different stroke orders are represented.

Try writing the characters in the boxes with the correct stroke order, then look on the right and check them.

Use a book to cover up the right side of the dotted line.

人
rén
person

日
rì
sun

山
shān
mountain

水
shuǐ
water

鸟
niǎo
bird

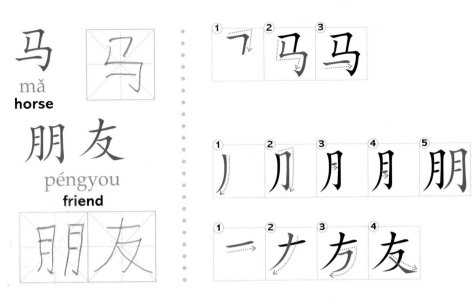

马
mǎ
horse

朋 友
péngyou
friend

Did you get any right? Well done if you did, but don't worry if you didn't. This is an aspect of learning Chinese that will eventually become second nature. Just concentrate on following the stroke orders in this book.

Picture it!

The original characters, written over 2,000 years ago, were pictures of things and some Chinese characters to this day are pictographs. Drawing on characters (whether they are pictographs or not) is a good way to help you to remember them.

Draw on these characters. *Look at the example.*

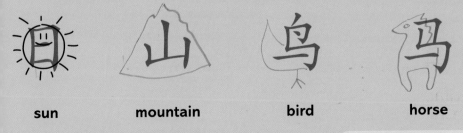

sun   **mountain**   **bird**   **horse**

It's radical

Some characters can be found making up parts of other characters. These characters then become 'radicals'. There are 214 radicals in total, and they can give clues to meaning and pronunciation.

To start you off, practise writing these four:

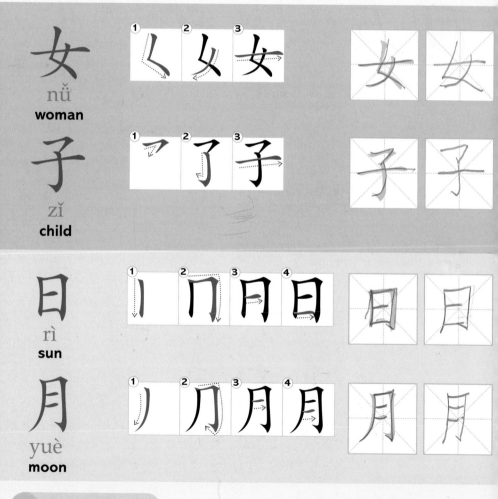

女
nǚ
woman

子
zǐ
child

日
rì
sun

月
yuè
moon

Notice how the meanings of the new characters directly relate to the meanings of the original characters.

Like building blocks, you put the characters together to make new ones.

好

hǎo
good

(literally woman and child together)

明

míng
bright

(literally sun and moon together)

明明
Bright Bright

Character practice 1

Practise writing the characters from this section here.

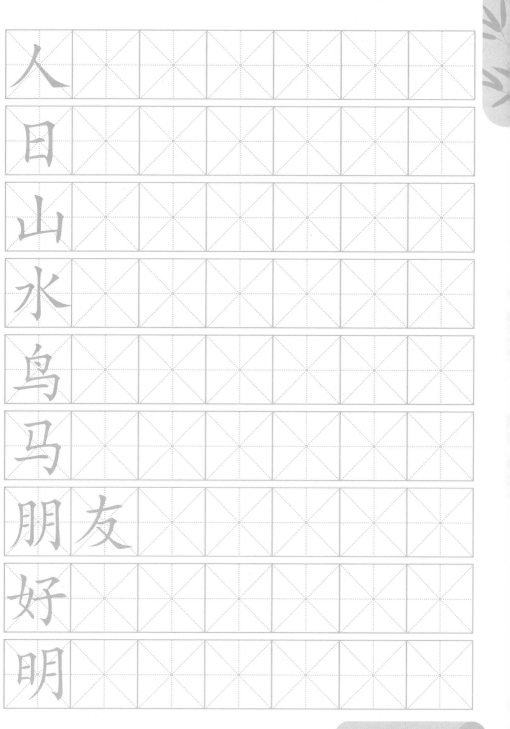

人

日

山

水

鸟

马

朋 友

好

明

First words

These are among the first words to learn in any language.

nǐ hǎo

hello

Copy the pinyin here:

nǐhǎo nǐhǎo

How to write it:

Your turn:

谢 谢　再 见

xièxie
thank you

zàijiàn
goodbye

Your turn:

Your turn:

Fill in the speech bubbles. What's the person saying?
Answers on page 128.

How are you?

Asking 'how are you?' is a good way to greet people in China, too.

First of all, learn these pronouns.

wǒ

I

How to write it:

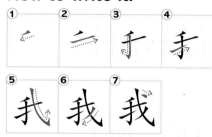

Your turn:

nǐ

you

How to write it:

Your turn:

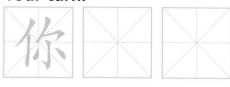

Hello + 'ma'

To say 'how are you?', simply add 'ma' to nǐ hǎo.

Nǐ hǎo ma?

How are you?

Your turn:

Copy the pinyin here:

Nǐ hǎo ma

I'm very well.

Now answer the question.

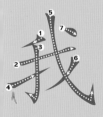 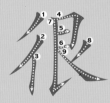 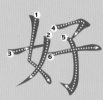

Wǒ hěn hǎo.

I'm very well.

Copy the pinyin here:

wǒ hěn hǎo

Your turn:

Where is it?

Being able to ask where things are will help you to find your way in China.

First learn these key characters.

zài nǎr...?

where is...?

Copy the pinyin here:

zài nǎr

How to write it:

Your turn:

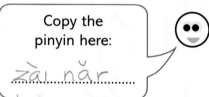

Now ask the way

To ask where something is, you simply add 'zài nǎr?' to the word for what you are looking for. For example: **Fàndiàn** means restaurant. **Fàndiàn zài nǎr?** means 'Where's the restaurant?' (this literally means 'Restaurant at where?').

Ask where each of these places are, using pinyin. Remember to put the noun first! *Answers on page 128.*

1

饭店
fàndiàn
restaurant

Where is the restaurant?

....

2

书店
shūdiàn
bookshop

Where is the bookshop?

....

3

茶馆
cháguǎn
tea house

Where is the tea house?

....

4

厕所
cèsuǒ
toilet

Where are the toilets?

....

Ladies and gents

The characters for 'man' and 'woman' are useful to know, especially as they are the toilet signs in China.

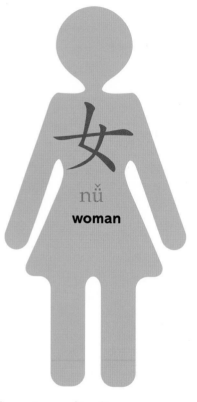

nǚ

woman

Picture it

Draw a head, hands, and shoes on the character to help you to remember it.

 The pinyin for 'nü' has two dots above the 'u'. This indicates a round 'ooo' sound.

How to write it:

① ② ③

Your turn:

Three characters for the price of one

The character for 'man' is made up of two other characters:

田	+	力	=	男
tián		lì		nán
field		**strength**		**man**

Together they literally mean 'strength in the field'. When the character was invented, over 2000 years ago, most men worked in paddy fields.

nán

man

Memory tip!
Change the 'm' in 'man' to an 'n' and you get 'nan'!

How to write it:

Your turn:

Welcome!

Give a warm welcome by inviting someone in for a nice cup of tea.

qǐng

please

(pronounced 'ching')

How to write it:

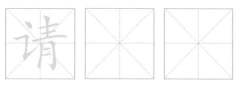

Your turn:

Fill in the spaces with one (or two) of these characters in the boxes. *Answers on page 128.*

进　喝茶　坐

1

Please come in!

Your turn:

请 !

 jìn
to enter

 zuò
to sit

Your turn:

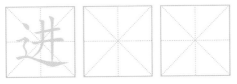

Your turn:

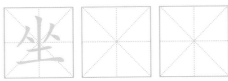

 hē
to drink

 chá
tea

Your turn:

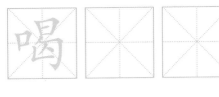

Your turn:

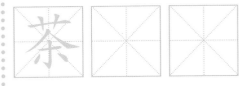

2 Please sit down!

3 Please have a cup of tea.

Your turn:

Your turn:

What's your name?

Learn how to reply when someone asks you what your name is.

jiào

to be called

How to write it:

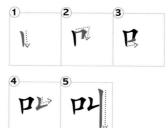

Your turn:

Nǐ jiào shénme?

What's your name?

Your turn:

Wǒ jiào Wáng Yīng.

I'm called Wang Ying.

Wang is a common surname. Note: surnames come first in China.

Ying is a common given name and means 'brave'.

Your turn:

Answer the question using pinyin and your own name.

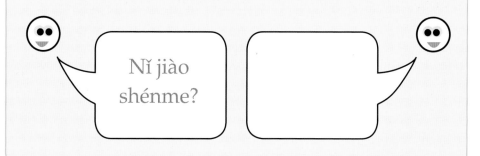

Nǐ jiào shénme?

Character practice 2

Practise the characters from this section here.

饭店
书店
茶馆
厕所
女
男
请
进
坐

More to do!

Keep going. This section includes these, too...

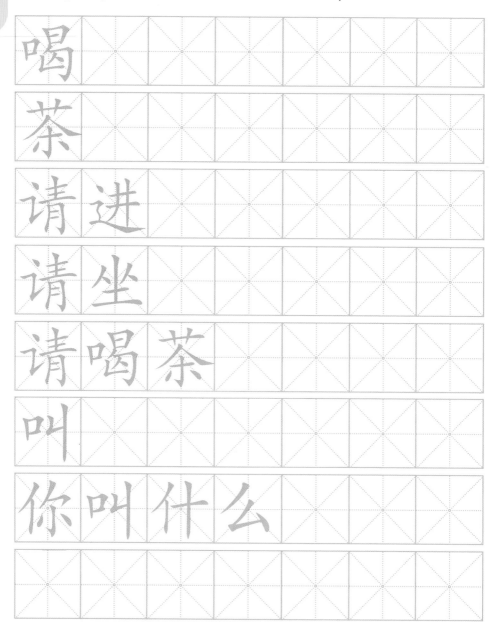

喝

茶

请 进

请 坐

请 喝 茶

叫

你 叫 什 么

Practice squares

Extra space for extra practice.

Head...

These next pages include body vocabulary, starting at the top.

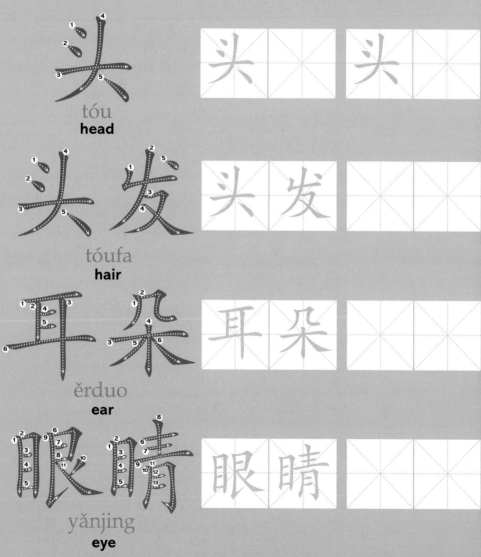

tóu
head

tóufa
hair

ěrduo
ear

yǎnjing
eye

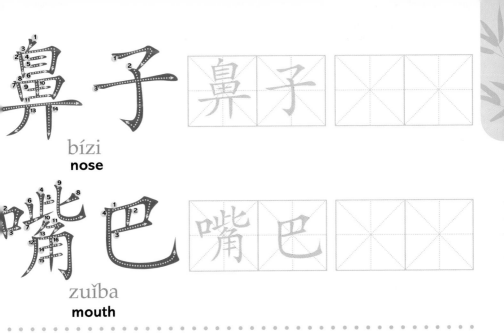

bízi
nose

zuǐba
mouth

Label the girl's head with the correct characters, or pinyin... or both! Whichever you prefer.

...to tail

Copy the Chinese characters for the parts of the body.

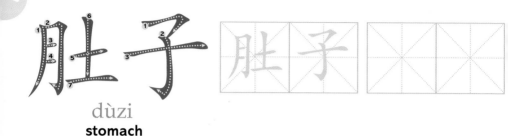

dùzi
stomach

gēbo
arm

shǒu
hand

tuǐ
leg

jiǎo

foot

Label the lady.

Sizing things up

Here are two easy peasy characters to learn: big and small.

dà

big

Picture it

The character for 'big' looks like a man with outstretched arms. Draw on hands and a head.

Copy the pinyin here:

....

How to write it:

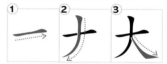

Your turn:

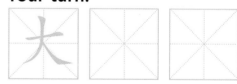

Big or small?

Write whether the objects are big or small in Chinese characters. *Answers on page 128.*

1

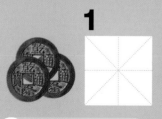

2

Itty bitty things

With Chinese characters, small details matter. For example, 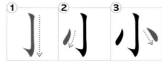, take note of the little dots each side, and the little flick up to the left on the down stroke.

Remember, all Chinese characters take up the same amount of space on the paper and there is an equal distance between each one.

学习中文很有意思。中文的字很漂亮。我喜欢学习中文。你呢?

xiǎo

small

(pronounced 'sh-yaow')

How to write it:

① ② ③

Your turn:

Copy the pinyin here:

....

3

4

De-der!

This character is the most common character in Chinese. Its meaning isn't too glamorous. It's the possessive particle.

No.1

de
[possessive particle]

How to write it:

Your turn:

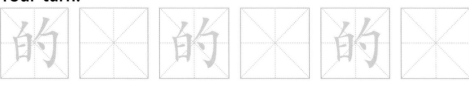

'De' can be added to just about anything as a connector. It shows possession. For example, in English, an apostrophe 's' is used: 'the ship's cat' means 'the cat that belongs to the ship'. In Chinese, 'de' is used, so you would say, 'ship **de** cat'. That is why it is so common.

'I' into 'my'

Here 'de' is used to make 'I' into 'my', and 'you' into 'your'.

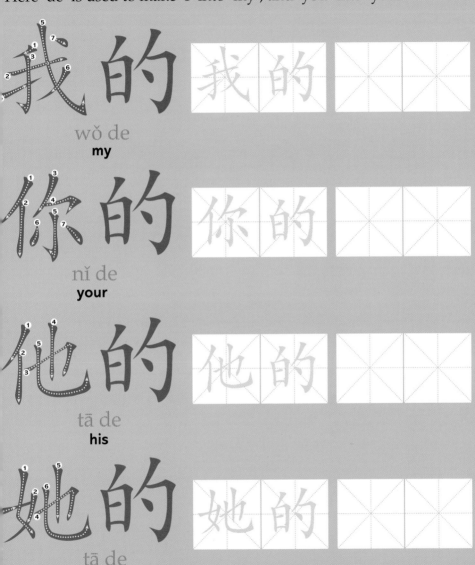

我 的
wǒ de
my

你 的
nǐ de
your

他 的
tā de
his

她 的
tā de
her

'Tā de' (his) and 'tā de' (her) differ only in their characters.
Note that the 'woman' radical makes the difference.

Meet the family

There are two words for brother and two for sister depending on whether older or younger.

māma
mother

bàba
father

mèimei
younger sister

jiějie
older sister

dìdi
younger brother

gēge
older brother

Making introductions

Knowing how to introduce someone is polite and useful.

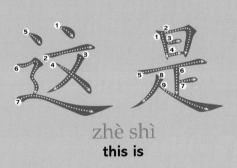

zhè shì
this is

Your turn:

Put these words together to introduce a family member.

For example:

Zhè shì + wǒ de + mèimei.

= This is my younger sister.

Write 'This is my mother.' in pinyin here:

Answer on page 128.

Character practice 3

Practise writing the characters from this section here.

脚
手
腿
大
小
的
我　的
你　的
他　的

More to do!

Keep going. This section includes these, too...

她 的

妈 妈

爸 爸

妹 妹

姐 姐

弟 弟

哥 哥

这 是

Practice squares

Extra space for extra practice.

The Middle Kingdom

In ancient times, the regions around China paid tribute to the Chinese Emperor, and China came to be called the Middle Kingdom.

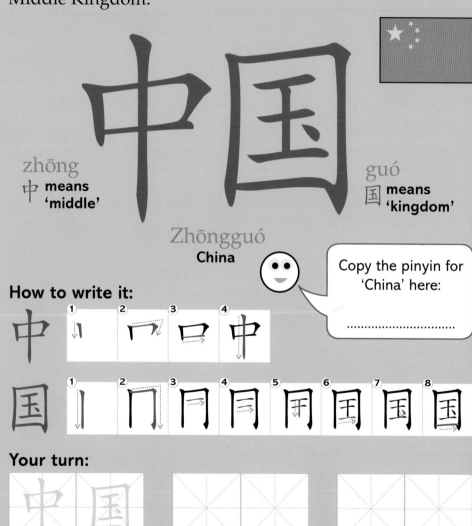

zhōng
中 means 'middle'

guó
国 means 'kingdom'

Zhōngguó
China

Copy the pinyin for 'China' here:

....

How to write it:

Your turn:

A character with legs

The character for 'person' is an ancient pictogram and looks like two legs walking.

How to write it:

Picture it! Draw a head and feet on the character to help you remember it.

rén
person

Your turn:

Simply add 'rén' to 'Zhōngguó' to say 'Chinese person'.

中国人

Zhōngguórén
Chinese person

Your turn:

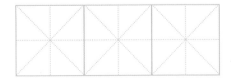

Countries of the world

In Chinese, the names of other countries are translated using characters with the appropriate sound. Or they can be literal translations, in the case of Japan.

Translating the characters gives interesting, and flattering, results. Some country names are purely phonetic, however, as with 'Holland' (the Netherlands).

Měiguó **USA (beautiful country)**

Yīngguó **Britain (brave country)**

Fǎguó **France (legal country)**

德国 Déguó **Germany (virtuous country)**

日本 Rìběn **Japan (rising sun)**

荷兰 Hélán **Netherlands (phonetic Holland)**

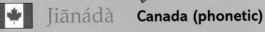

加拿大 Jiānádà **Canada (phonetic)**

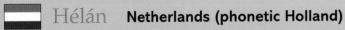

Where are you from?

This is the question strangers in China will ask you before any other.

ně

which

How to write it:

Your turn:

Copy the question and answer in the boxes provided.

你 是 哪 国 人？

Nǐ shì nǎ guó rén?   **Which country are you from?**

我 是 英 国 人。

Wǒ shì Yīngguórén.   **I am British.**

Geography test

Look back a page at the countries' names and have a go at labelling the globe using pinyin. *Answers on page 128.*

1

2

3

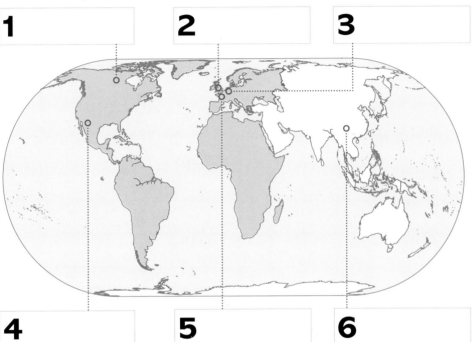

4

5

6

Your turn

Translate from English into pinyin.
Answers on page 128.

> Remember, by adding 'rén' to the country's name you are saying 'people' of that country.

1 Where are you from? ....

2 I am British. ....

3 I am French. ....

4 I am Japanese. ....

Character practice 4

Practise writing the characters from this section here.

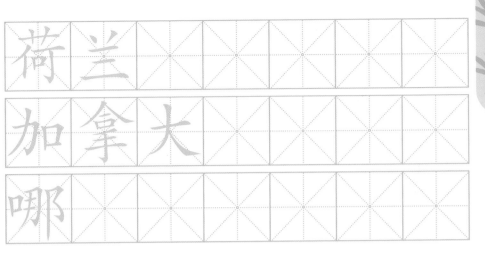

Practice squares

Extra space for extra practice.

Numbers 1–10

Learning numbers 1–10 is simple and very useful. The characters for numbers 1–3 are the easiest of them all.

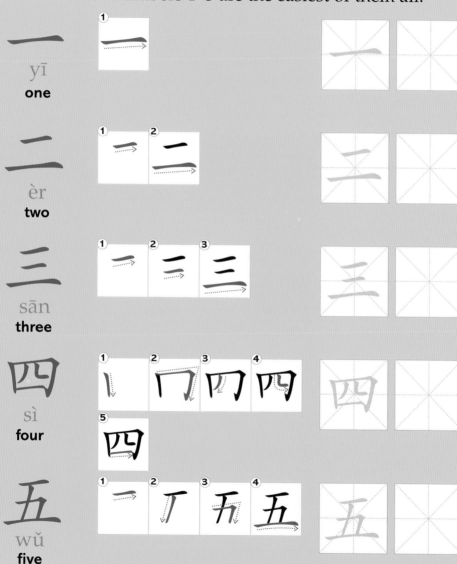

yī
one

èr
two

sān
three

sì
four

wǔ
five

六
liù
six

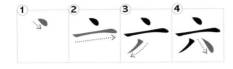

七
qī
seven

八
bā
eight

九
jiǔ
nine

十
shí
ten

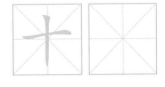

10 to a million

To count above 10, it takes some simple maths.

- If a number comes *after* 10 (十), you *add* it to 10.
- If a number comes *before* 10 (十), you *times* it by 10.

How it works...

十三	shísān	13	3 *after* 10 so that means 10 + 3
三十	sānshí	30	3 *before* 10 so that means 3 x 10
三十二	sānshíèr	32	2 *after* and 3 *before* 10 so that means (3 x 10) + 2

What are these numbers? *Answers on page 128.*

1 十五 ☐

5 二十三 ☐

2 四十 ☐

6 七十一 ☐

3 十八 ☐

7 九十九 ☐

4 十四 ☐

8 五十八 ☐

100 +

Higher numbers string together in the same way, with 10, 100 and 1,000 acting as 'stops'. Practise writing the number words, then have a go at the maths test below.

bǎi
100

qiān
1,000

wàn
10,000

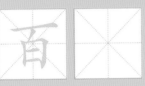

Look at these numbers as an example:

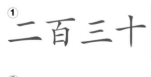   sìbǎisānshí   430

   sānqiānèrbǎi   3,200

    wǔwàn   50,000

Maths test
Do you know what these numbers say? *Answers on page 128.*

①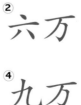

② 六万

③ 四千三百

④ 九万

Days of the week

Here numbers 1–6 count out the days of the week.

xīngqī

weekday
(pronounce this 'shingchee')

How to write it:

星

| ① ヽ | ② 冂 | ③ 口 | ④ 日 | ⑤ 旦 | ⑥ 旦 | ⑦ 旱 | ⑧ 旱 |

| ⑨ 星 |

期

| ① 一 | ② 十 | ③ 廿 | ④ 廿 | ⑤ 甘 | ⑥ 其 | ⑦ 其 | ⑧ 其 |

| ⑨ 其 | ⑩ 期 | ⑪ 期 | ⑫ 期 |

Your turn:

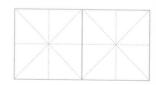

Once you know how to write 'weekday' in Chinese, you add the numbers 1–6 to get Monday (literally 'weekday 1') to Saturday ('weekday 6'). Only Sunday is different.

Monday xīngqīyī	星 期 一
Tuesday xīngqīèr	星 期 二
Wednesday xīngqīsān	星 期 三
Thursday xīngqīsì	星 期 四
Friday xīngqīwǔ	星 期 五
Saturday xīngqīliù	星 期 六
Sunday xīngqītiān	星 期 天

Months of the year

Once you've learnt the basic numbers, it's also really easy to learn the months of the year.

First learn this character, which is a pictograph of the moon.

yuè
moon/month

Copy the pinyin here:

....

Picture it
Draw on the character and turn it into a crescent moon.

How to write it:

Your turn:

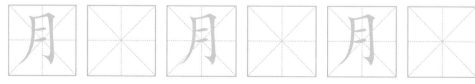

January
一月
yīyuè

February
二月
èryuè

March
三月
sānyuè

April
四月
sìyuè

May
五月
wǔyuè

June
六月
liùyuè

July
七月
qīyuè

August
八月
bāyuè

September
九月
jiǔyuè

October
十月
shíyuè

November
十一月
shíyīyuè

December
十二月
shíèryuè

Birthday party

Nowadays, people in China are likely to celebrate their birthdays with a cake and by singing 'Happy Birthday' (in Mandarin of course).

生 日 快 乐!

Shēngrì kuàilè!

Happy Birthday!

How to write it:

生 ① ✓ ② ✓ ③ ✓ ④ 牛 ⑤ 生

日 ① │ ② 冂 ③ 日 ④ 日

快 ① ✓ ② 丨 ③ 忄 ④ 忄 ⑤ 忄 ⑥ 快 ⑦ 快

乐 ① ✓ ② 二 ③ 千 ④ 牙 ⑤ 乐

Your turn:

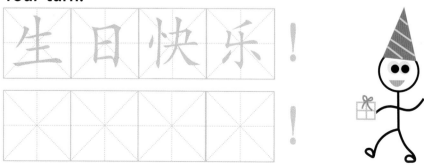

How old are you?

There are two ways to ask this question in Chinese. The first is for adults and older children:

Nǐ duō dà?
How old are you?

Your turn:

The second is for children under ten:

你几岁？

Nǐ jǐ suì?
How old are you?

Answer the question using your number knowledge by inserting your age in the space provided.

我 .... 岁。
Wǒ............. suì.

I'm .... years old.

Character practice 5

Practise writing the characters from this section here.

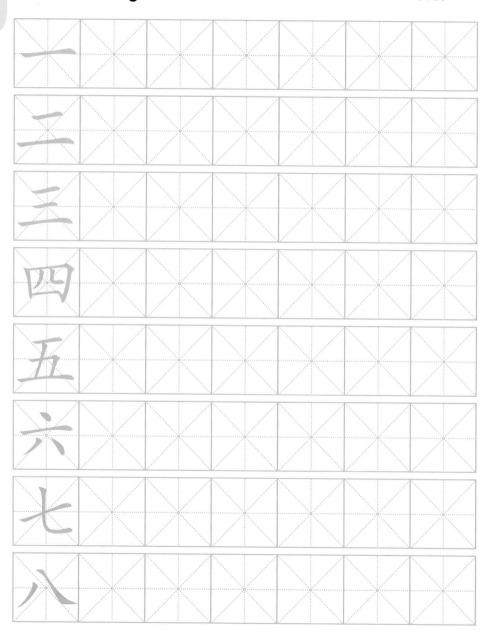

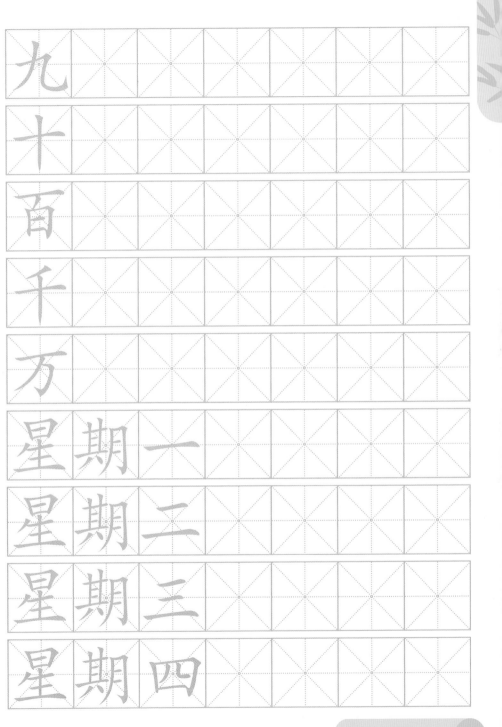

九

十

百

千

万

星 期 一

星 期 二

星 期 三

星 期 四

More to do!

Keep going. This section includes these, too...

星期五

星期六

星期天

一月

二月

三月

四月

五月

六月

七月

八月

九月

十月

十一月

十二月

生日快乐

North to south

China is big and major cities experience different weather.

北

běi

north

How to write it:

① ② ③ ④ ⑤

Your turn:

Beijing (literally meaning 'northern capital') is in north China. It's hot in the summer, and below freezing in winter.

东

dōng

east

How to write it:

① ② ③ ④ ⑤

Your turn:

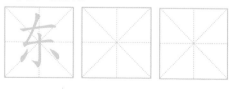

Shanghai is in the east. It has a warm spring, a hot, rainy summer, a cool autumn, and a cold winter.

南

nán
south

How to write it:

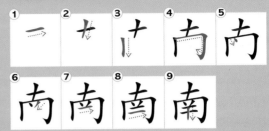

Your turn:

Guangzhou (Canton) is in the south. It has warm winters and hot, humid summers.

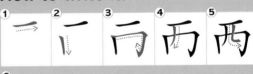

西

xī
west

How to write it:

Your turn:

Chengdu is in the west. It's warm in spring, sultry in summer, rainy in autumn, and the winter is cold.

Seasons

The seasons in China vary
depending on where you are.

**First learn the character common to them all,
then practise writing the seasons in the boxes.**

tiān
day/heaven

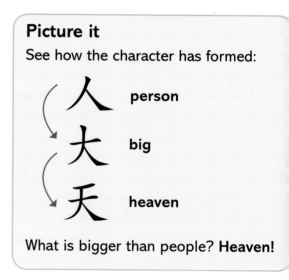

Picture it
See how the character has formed:

人 **person**

大 **big**

天 **heaven**

What is bigger than people? **Heaven!**

How to write it:

Your turn:

Copy the pinyin
here:

....

chūntiān **spring**

春天

xiàtiān **summer**

夏天

qiūtiān **autumn**

秋天

dōngtiān **winter**

冬天

Weather words

Find out the weather forecast... in Chinese.

热

rè

hot

How to write it:

Your turn:

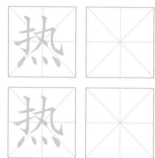

冷

lěng

cold

How to write it:

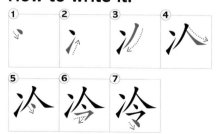

Your turn:

下雨

xià yǔ

rainy

(pronounced 'shar yoo')

How to write it:

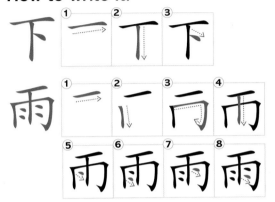

Your turn:

刮风

guā fēng

windy

(pronounced 'guh-wah fung')

How to write it:

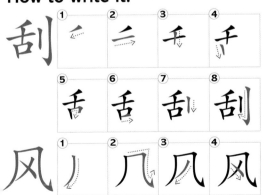

Your turn:

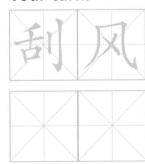

Character practice 6

Practise writing the characters from this section here.

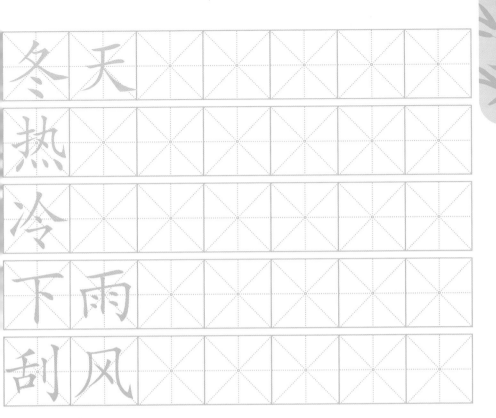

Practice squares

Extra space for extra practice.

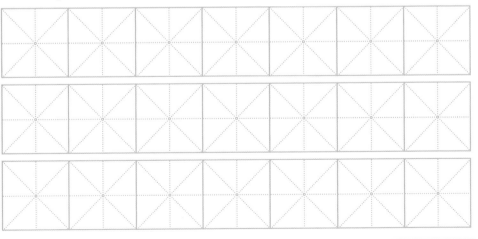

Traffic report

Knowing the words for 'car', 'bus' and 'train' is useful when travelling on China's public transport system.

First learn this character:

chē

vehicle
(pronounced 'ch-uh')

> Copy the pinyin here:
> ....

Picture it

This character was originally a pictograph of a horse-drawn cart (as seen from above).

seal script

old style character

new character used in China today

How to write it:

Your turn:

Traffic jam

All these means of transport have 'che' meaning 'vehicle' at the end. 'Aeroplane' is the exception. ('Feiji' literally means 'flying machine'.)

飞机

fēijī

aeroplane

zìxíngchē

bicycle

(pronounced 'z-uh shing ch-uh')

Your turn:

huǒchē

train

Your turn:

qìchē

car

Your turn:

出租车

chūzūchē

taxi

beep!

公共汽车

gōnggòngqìchē

bus

Finding the way

Make being lost in China a thing of the past with these useful words.

qǐngwèn

excuse me

Your turn:

zuǒbiān

left

Your turn:

yòubiān

right

Your turn:

Your turn:

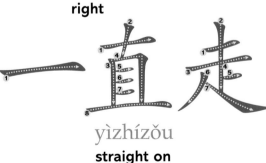

yìzhízǒu

straight on

Give directions

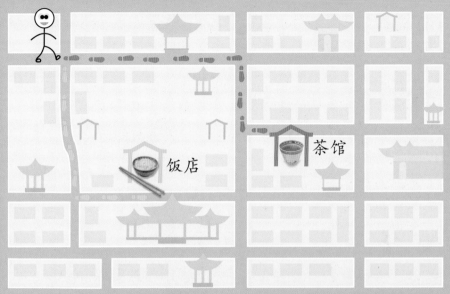

Have a go at giving directions to the lost tourist. Number the directions in the right order. *Answers on page 128.*

1 请问。饭店在哪儿?

Qǐngwèn. Fàndiàn zài nǎr?

Excuse me. Where is the restaurant?

yòubiān ☐   yìzhízǒu ☐   zuǒbiān ☐

2 请问。茶馆在哪儿?

Qǐngwèn. Cháguǎn zài nǎr?

Excuse me. Where is the tea shop?

zuǒbiān ☐   yòubiān ☐   yìzhízǒu ☐

Telling the time

If you are going somewhere, you will need to know what time your bus or train is leaving.

Follow these three rules:

1 Add **'diǎn'** to a number to say **'o'clock'**
For example, **'sān diǎn'** is **'three o'clock'**

2 Add **'diǎn bàn'** to say **'half past'**
For example, **'sān diǎn bàn'** is **'half past three'**

3 Add however many **'fēn'** (minutes) to make other times. For example, **'sān diǎn èrshí fēn'** is **'3:20'** – literally **'3 o'clock, 20 minutes'**

Practise the new characters first.

diǎn
o'clock

Your turn:

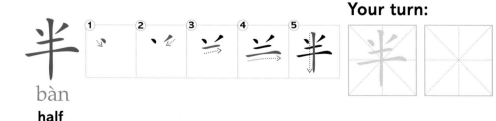

bàn
half

Your turn:

分

fēn

minute

Now try and tell the time on the clocks. Follow the example. *Answers on page 128.*

1

sān diǎn bàn

2

3

4

Buying a ticket

Asking to buy a ticket is the final step.

I want to buy a ticket to Beijing.

Here's how to ask:

我想买票。去北京。

Wǒ xiǎng mǎi piào. Qù Běijīng.

Here is the vocabulary broken down. Practise each word individually in the boxes.

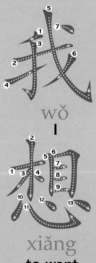

wǒ
I

Your turn:

xiǎng
to want

Your turn:

mǎi
to buy

Your turn:

piào
ticket

Your turn:

qù
to go

Your turn:

Běijīng
Beijing

Your turn:

Now put the words together (note there are two sentences in Chinese).

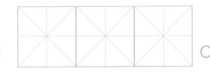

Here are the simple answers you can expect to hear.

没有。Méi yǒu.
I haven't got one.
(pronounced 'may yo')

有。Yǒu.
I have one.
(pronounced 'yo')

Character practice 7

Practise the characters from this section here.

车

自行车

火车

汽车

请问

左边

右边

一直走

点

半

分

我

想

买

票

去

北京

Chopsticks and bowl

When in China, eating with chopsticks is the norm.

kuàizi

chopsticks

How to write it:

筷

子

Your turn:

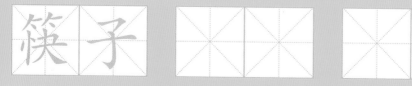

Your turn:

wǎn
bowl

sháozi
spoon

Your turn:

dāo
knife

Your turn:

chā
fork

Table talk

Impress people at your next Chinese meal by knowing some useful foodie phrases.

Hěn hǎo chī!

It's delicious!

Your turn:

| 很 | 好 | 吃 | ！ |

| | | | ！ |

Copy the pinyin here:

....

....

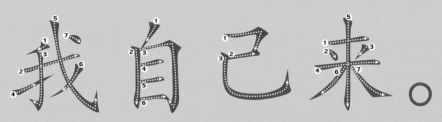

Wǒ zìjǐ lái.

I'll help myself.

Your turn:

我	自	己	来

Copy the pinyin here:

....

....

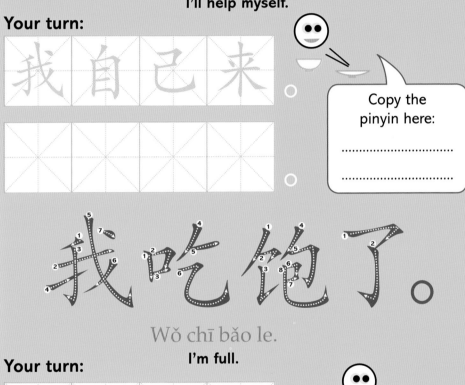

Wǒ chī bǎo le.

I'm full.

Your turn:

我	吃	饱	了

Copy the pinyin here:

....

....

Reading a menu

Look at the menu and choose a delicious dish.

Copy the characters.

Your turn:

米饭

mǐfàn

rice

Your turn:

面条

miàntiáo

noodles

Your turn:

蔬菜

shūcài

vegetables

yú

fish

jī

chicken

shuǐguǒ

fruit

diǎnxīn

dim sum

Restaurant words

You've chosen what you want to eat, now you need to communicate with the waiter.

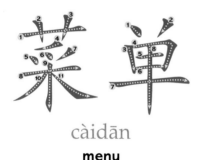

fúwùyuán

waiter/waitress

Your turn:

càidān

menu

Your turn:

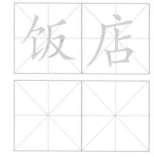

fàndiàn

restaurant

Your turn:

măidān

bill

chī

to eat

想

xiăng

to want

Look at the speech bubble. Can you guess what he is saying? *Answer on page 128.*

'Fúwùyuán, wŏ xiăng chī diănxīn.'

....

....

Character practice 8

Practise the characters from this section here.

筷子

碗

勺子

刀

叉

很好吃

我自己来

我 吃 饱 了

米 饭

面 条

蔬 菜

鱼

鸡

水 果

点 心

More to do!

Keep going. This section includes these, too...

服务员

菜单

饭店

买单

吃

想

Practice squares

Extra space for extra practice!

Hobbies

As well as learning Chinese, you may have other hobbies.

huàhuà
painting

Your turn:

tīng yīnyuè
listening to music

Your turn:

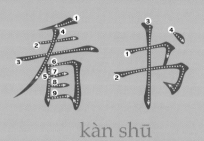

kàn shū

reading
(pronounced 'kan shoo')

Your turn:

xuéxí Zhōngwén

learning Chinese
(pronounced 'shoo-ay-shee jong-wen')

Your turn:

Ball games

Sport is an important part of life in China, with football and basketball being the most popular.

First learn this key character:

qiú

ball
(pronounced 'chee-oo')

How to write it:

Copy the pinyin here:

....

Your turn:

网球
wǎngqiú
tennis

Your turn:

网球

足球
zúqiú
football

Your turn:

足球

籃球
lánqiú
basketball

Your turn:

籃球

乒乓球 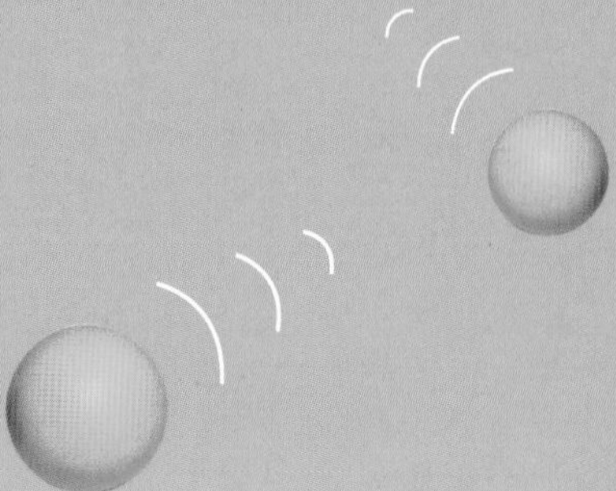
pīngpāngqiú
table tennis

Your turn:

乒乓球

Like it/love it

Learn how to say 'I love you' in Chinese.

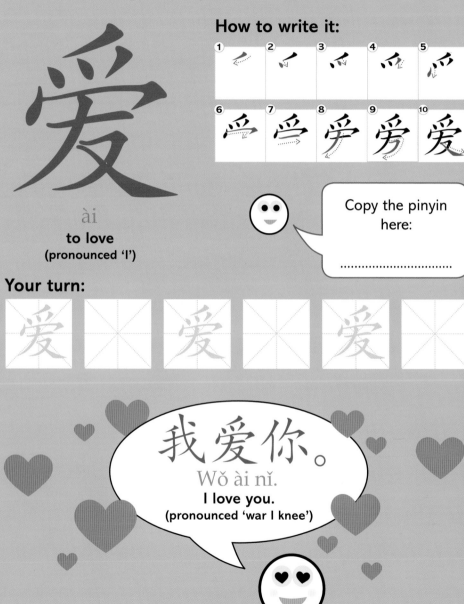

爱

ài
to love
(pronounced 'I')

How to write it:

| 1 | 2 | 3 | 4 | 5 |
| 6 | 7 | 8 | 9 | 10 |

Copy the pinyin here:

....

Your turn:

爱　　爱　　爱

我 爱 你。
Wǒ ài nǐ.
I love you.
(pronounced 'war I knee')

Saying 'boo'

Now learn how to say you like, or don't like, things.

First practise writing these characters:

xǐhuan
to like
(pronounced 'shee-hoo-an')

Your turn:

bù
not/no
(pronounced 'boo')

Your turn:

To say you like a sport you say:

我喜欢乒乓球。

Wǒ **xǐhuan** pīngpāngqiú.

I like table tennis.

To say you 'don't like' something, you add 'bù' in front of the verb:

我不喜欢网球。

Wǒ **bù xǐhuan** wǎngqiú.

I don't like tennis.

Character practice 9

Practise the characters from this section here.

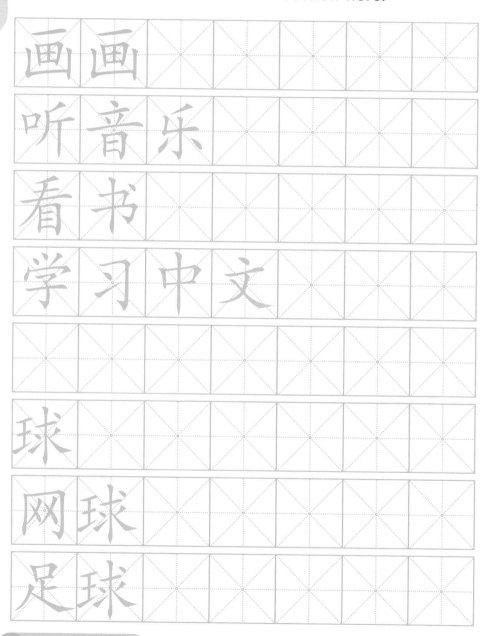

画画

听音乐

看书

学习中文

球

网球

足球

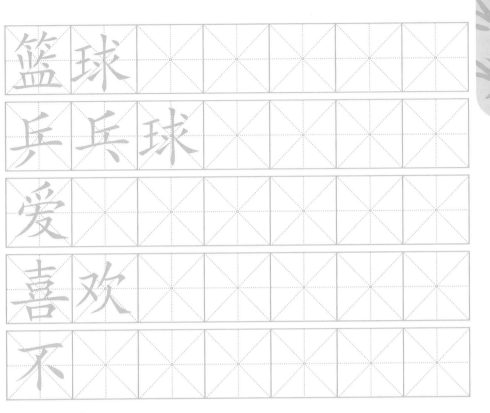

Practice squares

Extra space for extra practice.

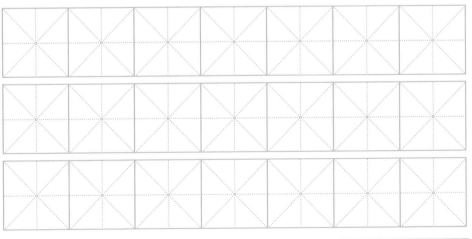

Beijing

The thriving capital city of China is home to beautiful palaces and a hundred-acre city square. Around Beijing, you can see…

kàn

to see

Picture it

看 kàn 'to see' includes a hand above an eye, as though shielding your eyes from the sun.

How to write it:

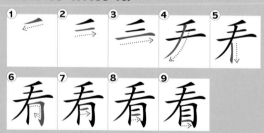

Your turn:

长城

Chángchéng

The Great Wall

Your turn:

长城

故宫

Gùgōng

The Forbidden City

Your turn:

故宫

天安门广场

Tiān'ānmén Guǎngchǎng

Tiananmen Square

Your turn:

天安门广场

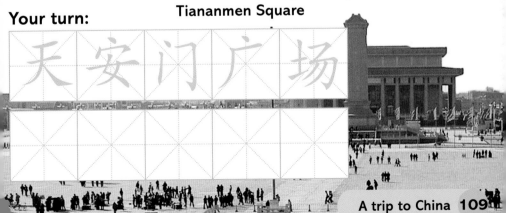

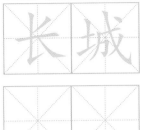

A day in the country

China is not all big cities. It has a beautiful and varied countryside.

First learn the characters for morning and afternoon.

Your turn:

shàngwǔ
morning

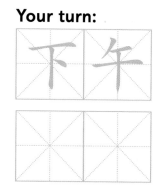

Your turn:

xiàwǔ
afternoon

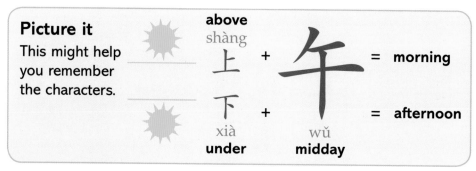

Picture it
This might help you remember the characters.

above
shàng
上 + 午 = morning

下 + = afternoon

xià   wǔ
under   **midday**

Plan your day

Now say what you are going to do in the morning and afternoon.

Write the characters in the boxes.

Morning 上午

páshān
climb a mountain

Your turn:

Afternoon 下午

zuò chuán
take a boat ride

Your turn:

qí mǎ
ride a horse

Your turn:

Useful phrases

These phrases will help you get by in China.

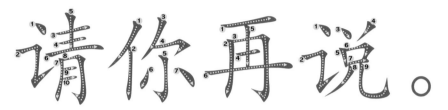

Qǐng nǐ zài shuō.

Please can you say it again.
(pronounced 'ching knee z-eye sh-war')

Your turn:

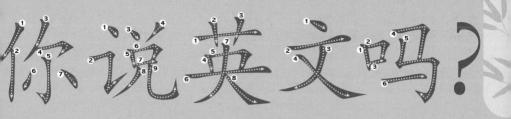

Nǐ shuō Yīngwén ma?

Do you speak English?

Your turn:

你 说 英 文 吗 ?

?

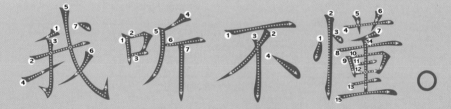

Wǒ tīng bù dǒng.

I don't understand.

Your turn:

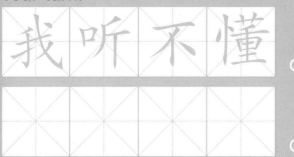 

Shopping list

Need some souvenirs? Time to go shopping!

pǐn

thing / article

Getting the stroke order right for boxes is useful as they often appear in Chinese characters.

Picture it

The character shows three containers. Draw some things you would like to buy in the boxes.

How to write it:

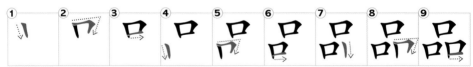

Your turn:

Here are some things you might buy:

Your turn:

sīzhīpǐn

silk
(pronounced 'suh-juh-pin')

Your turn:

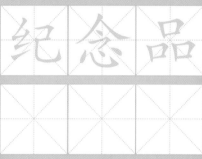

jìniànpǐn

souvenirs
(pronounced 'jee-nee-en-pin')

Your turn:

gōngyìpǐn

crafts

Festival!

If you are in China in late January or early February, you might be lucky and catch the Chinese New Year.

If so, you will definitely find this phrase useful to know.

Xīnnián kuàilè!

Happy New Year!

Your turn:

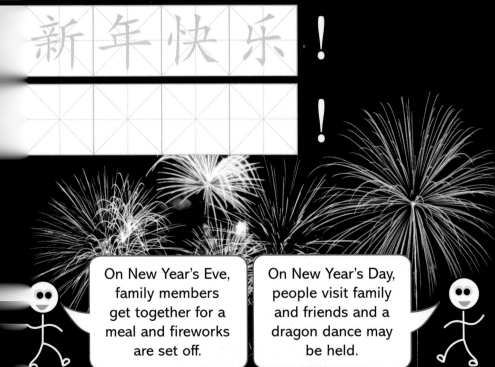

On New Year's Eve, family members get together for a meal and fireworks are set off.

On New Year's Day, people visit family and friends and a dragon dance may be held.

Let's party!

There are other major festivals in China.

Zhōng qiū jié
Mid-Autumn Festival

Your turn:

Duān wǔ jié
Dragon Boat Festival

Your turn:

Wherever you go, and whatever you do in China, have fun learning Mandarin Chinese!

Character practice 10

Practise the characters from this section here.

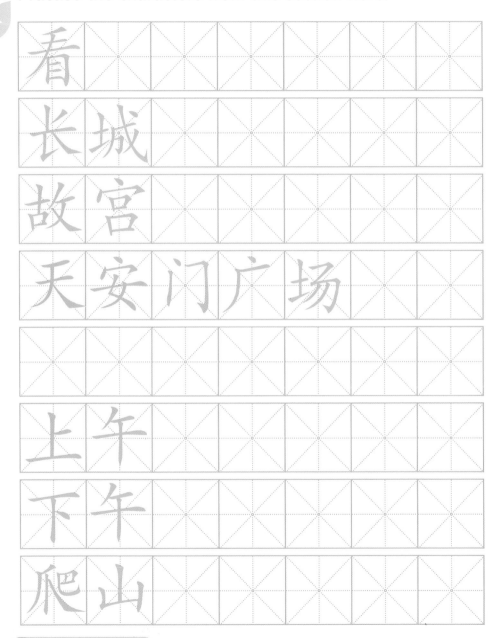

看

长 城

故 宫

天 安 门 广 场

上 午

下 午

爬 山

坐船

骑马

请你再说

你说英文吗

我听不懂

品

More to do!

Keep going. This section includes these, too...

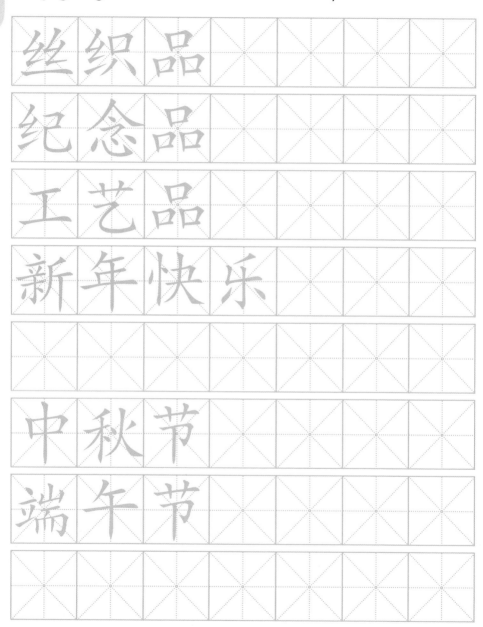

丝织品

纪念品

工艺品

新年快乐

中秋节

端午节

Practice squares

Extra space for extra practice.

Certificate

Congratulations to:

....

for successfully finishing this book.

好哇,干得漂亮!

Hǎo wa, gànde piàoliang!

Bravo! Well done!

Date:

Remember the golden rules of writing – if in doubt, write top to bottom, left to right!

....

Pronunciation guide

Pinyin is like a language all of its own. Use this rough guide to help you pronounce the words in this book.

Initial	Sound
b	baw
p	paw
m	maw
f	faw
d	duh
t	tuh
n	nuh
l	luh
g	guh
k	kuh
h	huh
j	gee

Initial	Sound
q	chee
x	she
z	dzuh
c	tsuh
s	suh
zh	jir
ch	chir
sh	shir
r	rj
w	ooh
y	ee

Final	Sound
a	ah
ai	i
ao	ow
an	ahn
ang	ahng
o	aw
ong	oong
ou	oh
e	uh
ei	ay
en	un
eng	ung

Final	Sound
er	ar
i	ee/uh
ia	ya
iao	yaow
ian	yan
iang	yahng
ie	yeh
in	een
ing	eeng
iong	yoong
iu	you
u	oo

Final	Sound
ua	wa
uo	waw
ui	way
uai	why
uan	won
un	un
uang	wahng
ü	yoo
ue	oo-weh
üan	ywan
ün	ywen

Useful words

Use this alphabetical list of words from the book for quick reference.

afternoon	xiàwǔ	下午
at	zài	在
autumn	qiūtiān	秋天
ball	qiú	球
basketball	lánqiú	篮球
bicycle	zìxíngchē	自行车
big	dà	大
birthday	shēngrì	生日
brother – older	gēge	哥哥
brother – younger	dìdi	弟弟
to buy	mǎi	买
car	qìchē	汽车
chicken	jī	鸡
China	Zhōngguó	中国
Chinese person	Zhōngguórén	中国人
chopsticks	kuàizi	筷子
cold	lěng	冷

dim sum	diǎnxīn	点心
to drink	hē	喝
east	dōng	东
to eat	chī	吃
to enter	jìn	进
father	bàba	爸爸
fish	yú	鱼
football	zúqiú	足球
fruit	shuǐguǒ	水果
to go	qù	去
goodbye	zàijiàn	再见
hello	nǐ hǎo	你好
hot	rè	热
I	wǒ	我
knife	dāo	刀
to like	xǐhuan	喜欢
to love	ài	爱
man	nánrén	男人
menu	càidān	菜单
moon	yuè	月

morning	shàngwǔ	上午
mother	māma	妈妈
no / not	bù	不
noodles	miàntiáo	面条
north	běi	北
to paint	huàhuà	画画
person	rén	人
please	qǐng	请
rain	yǔ	雨
restaurant	fàndiàn	饭店
rice	mǐfàn	米饭
to see	kàn	看
silk	sīzhīpǐn	丝织品
sister – older	jiějie	姐姐
sister – younger	mèimei	妹妹
to sit	zuò	坐
small	xiǎo	小
south	nán	南
souvenir	jìniànpǐn	纪念品
spoon	sháozi	勺子

spring	chūntiān	春天
to study	xuéxí	学习
summer	xiàtiān	夏天
table tennis	pīngpāngqiú	乒乓球
tea	chá	茶
tennis	wǎngqiú	网球
thank you	xièxie	谢谢
thing / article	pǐn	品
ticket	piào	票
toilet	cèsuǒ	厕所
train	huǒchē	火车
vehicle	chē	车
waiter	fúwùyuán	服务员
to want	xiǎng	想
west	xī	西
where	nǎr	哪儿
which	nǎ gè	哪个
winter	dōngtiān	冬天
woman	nǔrén	女人
you	nǐ	你

Answers

About the author

Elinor Greenwood graduated from Leeds University with a degree in Modern Chinese Studies. She has lived and worked in China for many years. She presently lives near Cambridge and divides her time between writing language books and teaching children Mandarin. She is the author of *Easy Peasy Chinese* and *Fun and Easy Chinese*.
Please see her website for more information:
www.noodlepublishing.com

Picture credits